DREAMERS' PARADISE

WRITERS POUCH

ISBN 979-888591870-1

Contents

Contents

Preface

Hello reader,

This book doesn't contain cover photos for all the poems published. Please visit our website writerspouch.com/book/16 to access the complete collection and appreciate all of our artists work. Thank you for your time, and we hope you enjoy our work.

- Writers Pouch Team

About "Beads"

One of the simplest objects that connect the rich, poor, ambitious, lazy, blessed, unfortunate or most individuals for that matter not just physically but even emotionally in our lives is beads. No matter who we are, where we come from or what we believe in, we are all connected by them.

"Beads" by Edlyn D'souza shows how individuals who seem to be radically different in their life or habits are in reality more alike than they think. It also shows how today's reality could be tomorrow's fantasy for any individual in this ever-changing world.

1. Beads

A queue of different beads
threaded together on a string.
All crafted to be unique and different,
holding presumptions of what each may bring.
A variety of shapes and colours…
…some found by chance, some lent by others.
The unfortunate, the downtrodden,
suffering from lack of a chance.
Ridden with pain and hunger,
pleading in a begging stance.
Reliving their daily fears…
…crying out beads of tears.

The labourers, the wage earners,
working hard for mere nothings.
Slogging through each day's work
and uncertainty the next one brings.
No dreams or hopes, only regret…
…losing life to beads of sweat.

The ambitious, the dreamers,
a cautiously optimistic lot.

Preparing for the best and worst,
when all to lose is all they've got.
Being led ahead by only hope as bait…
…chanting together on beads of faith.

The powerful, the influential,
those who make money move around.
They who fly in private jets,
whose feet needn't ever touch the ground.
Applauded for their generous charity…
…wearing beads of prosperity.

Doesn't matter where you come from,
we're all strung together like beads.
Constantly interchanging one for another,
through our daily deeds.
Not knowing which beads you'll hold tomorrow…
…unsure which ones bring joy, and which bring sorrow.

About "Be Yours?"

While many say a broken soul needs time to heal and the journey in this destination is dependent on the individual alone, there are others who say healing is impossible without the right person with an immense amount of faith, love and support standing by.

"Be Yours?" by Sahithi Mandapati expresses the thoughts of a passionate youngster trying to figure out if she can be the right person to heal a wounded soul and be his happiness too in order to lead a life together with him forever.

2. Be Yours?

Those eyes...
They look like a galaxy with a thousand stars
They look like they talk to your soul
They look like they are taking away your pain
When those eyes meet with yours...
Your mind stops every thought it has
Your heart jumps into a pool of happiness
Those eyes... an image which never leaves your soul
But behind those beautiful eyes
Lies sorrow which shines like stars
Lies endless doubts which are eating him away
Lies endless pain which is tearing his heart apart
Lies a longing for someone who will give him the happiness he deserves
Lies a beautiful heart with a broken soul
Those eyes are searching for...
Someone who can build him back
Someone who gives him everything he never had
Someone who gives a new meaning to his life
Someone who holds him like a child in her hands
Someone who puts his spirit back into his soul
Someone who medicates his wounded heart

Someone whose touch makes him feel like home
But
Can I be that someone in his life?
Can my eyes be the image in his soul?
Can I make him dance with me while his heartbeat becomes the music that's played?
Can I take his heart and mingle it with mine?
Can I talk to his soul and hear its cries?
Can I take his hand and lead him on a path that he never knew existed?
Can I guide him when he is lost?
Can I be... the One... to love him... Forever.

About "Delight"

Thanking God for his help in pointing the way, poet Rohit Damaraju mentions how he learnt the true reason for his existence following the divine path.

The poem "Delight" expresses a poet's gratitude for the help received in his time of need. It also states how this path offered a purpose rather than being lost in the abyss of ignorance.

3. Delight

Walking through the galore of life I found
Happiness, thrill, and strife without bounds

A lot of paths were there to trod
It was only me and my God

That instant, I thought
Let all the feelings in me
Be completely engrossed in there

The reason as to why?
I will tell you as I cry...
The pearls of happiness which roll from these eyes
Are because you pulled me into truth
From the turbid waters of lies
I was incomplete with cracks unseen
The labyrinth of reasons was cruel and mean

You completed the unsolved puzzle
Helped me fight my war with the muzzle
Now that I am unwavering
Focused for the reason you had me preferred,

I can see the world with a greater cause,
A velvety heart and rippling grit that you gave me because,
Let your touch prevail through my life
Over the world let delight strive.

About "Grey"

To watch age deteriorate and weaken the strongest persons you've known, is never easy. The slow suffocation caused by Time leaves us all gasping.

"Grey" by Manognya Bethapudi is an attempt at catharsis, an attempt to dissect feelings and to process them.

4. Grey

It was slow
Black and brown became grey
Laugh lines became deep creases
march became a tread
And you became alone
Two became one
A hollow shell of one

Curious eyes leached colour
Spry shoulders sagged under the weight
Of dragging your stars through the night
Full arms, fallen wide

I watched from the side
As your eyes clouded with age and grief
As your hands reached out to hold ether
As you held your pieces together with pain

I watched from the side
As they erased your reds
They took away your yellows
And blanketed you in white

I watched from the side
Another pair of eyes
In your deconstruction
In the unpacking of your essence

And I was silent
I was complicit in this violence

I saw everything
but never through your eyes

It was fast
It was too fast
That you were left all alone

About "My Anxiety Speaks to Me!"

Did you ever stay awake at night and feel your chest tightening while anxiety is slowly swallowing your sanity, observing humans exploit our world? Does it bother you that we ignore its well being and continue exploiting it until our beautiful habitat becomes horrifying to live on anymore?

"My Anxiety Speaks to Me!" by Nikhila Kotni illustrates how a little girl feels looking at the world slowly destroyed by her fellow human beings at the expense of their emotional drive and collective intellectual failure.

5. My Anxiety Speaks to Me!

Sometimes at night
When the world is fast asleep
I lay awake while my anxiety speaks to me

"Boundaries! Boundaries! Boundaries!"
My anxiety speaks to me!
Why do we have Boundaries?
Why do we have walls?
Why fight wars to defend these man-made Boundaries?

"Peace! Peace! Peace!"
My anxiety speaks to me!
Why do we have peace workers?
Why do we have peace awards?
Why do we have peace symbols but not peace?

"Trivial! Trivial! Trivial!"
My anxiety speaks to me!
Why seek world peace?
Why fight world hunger?

Why discuss Global warming?
To save humankind?
Why save humankind?

"Destroy! Destroy! Destroy!"
My anxiety speaks to me!
Humans destroyed multiple species,
Tigers, cranes, gorillas, marine life
Too many species on the brink of extinction
So millions of humans could live in luxury?

"Time! Time! Time!"
My anxiety speaks to me!
Turn back the time
The time before Humans
Chirping birds, dancing deers, roaring tigers and jumping dolphins
A world without humans, a world without boundaries
What a peaceful world it is!

About “Realisation”

Life is so mysterious that a few might not even realise its value or experience it in their entire lifetime. It is only a few who truly reach a point to realise its true value.

“Realisation” by Rohit Damaraju talks about existence, realisation, civilization and ignorance while mentioning how anyone who realises the power of existence is never the same again.

6. Realisation

Today, I realised that I existed,
from the whispers of life that I hated.
Today, I realised that I existed,
as a civilisation was spewed, when two souls mated.
You too will realise, beholder.
Just look at the magic in the pebble and the boulder.
The waves of binding creepers and whirlpools stir.
Flow yourself and blend.
Morrow, you'd realise that existence,
is the omnipresent network of past, present and future tense.
Someday will come when you will rise from this sleep.
Someday… the world would realise this matter so deeply.

About "Rower"

Writing about the life of a lonely rower, poet Santhosh Annabattula talks about how different people repay the rower when he drops them on the other shore before returning to his true home, the river water until sunset. The poem "Rower" illustrates the feelings of a rower on a sunny day.

7. Rower

I am a rower
Living by my boat
Paddling through life,
Wading through the waters
Sometimes rough, sometimes smooth
I carry people as my own
Some on the shore, some lost in the water
I take them to safety
To the far bank ashore
I carry them with care,
Listening to their stories
Cherishing every moment together
I row against the current
Against wind and storm alike
To carry people as my own..

When I leave them ashore
Some bid a fond farewell
Some just give me a smile
Some nod and go on their way
And some never look back
But I do what I do best

And go back to the waters
With thoughts like ripples,
Many people I meet
Yet I am always alone
As no one stays behind.
I am a lonely rower
Paddling through life
Without a shore to reach
As the ripples ebb away
I retreat into the sunset
After a hard day's work.

About "The Lonely Heart's Stupid Song"

Enthralled by the presence of his sweetheart, poet Rohit Damaraju describes his enchanting experience, relishing the beauty of the love of his life.

Filled with endearment, "The Lonely Heart's Stupid Song" is an emotionally written poem encompassing the poet's unending passion for a soulmate with a memorable and spell-binding rhythm in every verse.

8. The Lonely Heart's Stupid Song

The mist of mind clouds me,
As I see you glee,
Under the sparkling moonlight,
Beside the seashore and thicket of this night,
My heart retreats to your place,
Like a hungry tiger with a tremendous pace,
Oh! Please don't veil your face,
An epitome of vibrancy and grace…
Below this gleam, your lips velvety red,
A symmetrical vermilion seam on your forehead,
You are my yin and yang;
All this --- My heart sang,
Because, the waves of your existence,
Trilled my soul with a twang!

About "See You Tomorrow"

The covid pandemic hit us like a storm and overturned our world upside down. For overworked resident doctors in the fragile healthcare system, it meant worrying that each shift could be the last time they see a patient.

"See You Tomorrow" by Manognya Bethapudi is a plea by one such resident doctor begging her patients to hang in there while they try to figure out how to keep their patients alive for the next twenty-four hours.

9. See You Tomorrow

I masked my emotions
like I masked my face
My glasses fogged
with sweat or was it tears?
Day in and day out
I said to my patients
See you tomorrow
See you tomorrow

Every day I said
Just one more needle
Just one more machine
You will get better
And I'll see you tomorrow

Every day I did some
And tried some more
Like a raft on choppy waves
I kept going
Just to be able to say
See you tomorrow
See you tomorrow

I took home with me
The virus and its friends
Anxiety, insomnia
And a background score of beeps
Before leaving I always said
See you tomorrow
See you tomorrow

The beeps, they fumbled
So I rushed to your side
I gave my everything
and then some more
But then they fell silent
And now I won't
See you ever again.

About "Sinner"

What is identity without ego? Is it bad to seek a better life? Aren't all of us striving for comfort? What's wrong with some harmless lies? Should we be judged if we choose our own benefit? If so, why? Aren't all of us the same when it comes to desire?

"Sinner" by Santhosh Annabattula not only answers a few of these questions but also shows how individuals filled with greed and contentment of their deeds not only deflect the thought of introspection of their immoral actions but in fact, defend them.

10. Sinner

Let me tell you something
Can't say if this is a confession
Don't believe in heaven or hell either
All I wanted is my happiness
And to live as long as I can
"Who doesn't?", Echoes a voice
If there is someone to blame
Then it's this voice inside my head
Deviously inciting and tricking me

I have to admit I am selfish
Putting me above everything else
But isn't everyone the same?
Rings my inner voice with wisdom

I nurture my ego every day
And deny it at the same time
What's my identity without my ego?
Nods my inner voice in agreement

My ambitions border on greed
In craving for money and success

What's bad in the desire for a better life?
Demands my inner voice in anger

I envy all those undeserving people
And curse my rotten luck for it
Of course, life has not been fair to me
Rues my inner voice in resentment

My anger often boils over as rage
And hurt the people around me
But I deserve to vent out my emotions
Comforts my inner voice in solidarity

I get dishonest in some situations
To wriggle my way out of problems
What's wrong with some harmless lies?
Asserts my inner voice in conviction

I know what you are thinking
Come on now, don't start judging me
It's not like I committed a grave crime,
Haven't robbed a bank or killed people
Don't deserve any trial for my actions.
It is just me, my desires and my flaws
I am imperfect and I love the way I am
Let's pretend I never told you anything
And we will start all over again!

About "Survivor"

The human instinct to see a scary future, especially when facing their nemesis, is undoubtedly terrifying. But what they do when feeling this terror is their defining moment.

"Survivor" by Santhosh Annabattula narrates the thoughts of a survivor who is willing to fight to the end at the cost of existence. The poem ostensibly depicts even if the mortal form is unbroken, the survivor's spirit isn't.

11. Survivor

Are you a shadow?
Creeping behind my back
Are you the wisp of the wind?
Trying to sneak past my breath
Are you a sense of foreboding?
Trickling down my spine
Are you my nemesis?
Questioning my very existence
Are you my reckoning?
In this moment of truth
Are you the face of death?
An eventuality and a finality
Too small to behold; Too vast to understand

The drums are rolling,
The sky is lit in crimson
The lines have been drawn
In the battle of our generation
Fight I will, with all my strength
With my restraint and resilience
I do not see what lies ahead
In this clash for survival

But I do see what I am fighting
The darkness of my doubt and fear
I gather all my resolve
And look at the face
Of my mortal enemy
And vow not to give in

My body may be broken
But my spirit will not.

About "Whispers & Murmurs"

Two of the most frequently performed activities that are largely portrayed in a negative light are whispers and murmurs. Disrespected by many for being uttered by cowards or haters with little regard for the consequences of their actions, these activities are largely condemned.

Read "Whispers & Murmurs" by Edlyn D'souza to realise how these activities do not always necessarily fail everyone at all times but even nurture a few bonds if performed properly and cautiously.

12. Whispers & Murmurs

Giggling chuckles
in a kindergarten class.
"Pin drop silence!", is the command,
as little voices on heavy breaths
are passed from one desk to another.
Hushed teenage secrets
meant for just one ear.
That of a best friend, considered special
and dear that's how we learned
to trust and confide in another.

Campus gossips
spread through wagging tongues.
Changing narratives, edited descriptions -
that's how stories are scripted
to be sung through the words of another.

Professional accolades
often applauded on centre stage.
True competence or undeserved recognition

candidly gauged in the mumbles
that travel over shoulders about another.

About Poets

1. **Edlyn D'souza**

   Poet of "Beads" & "Whispers & Murmurs"

   Edlyn has been a member of the community since 2020 and she writes flash fiction & poems. Her works can be accessed at writerspouch.com/profile/41

2. **Manognya Bethapudi**

   Poet of "Grey" & "See You Tomorrow"

   Manognya has been a member of the community since 2014 and she writes poems & short stories. Her works can be accessed at writerspouch.com/profile/9

3. **Nikhila Kotni**

   Poet of "My Anxiety Speaks to Me!"

   Nikhila has been a member of the community since 2014 and she writes flash fiction & short stories. Her works can be accessed at writerspouch.com/profile/6

4. **Rohit Damaraju**

   Poet of "Delight", "Realisation" & "The Lonely Heart's Stupid

Song"

Rohit has been a member of the community since 2014 and he writes poems. His works can be accessed at writerspouch.com/profile/8

5. **Sahithi Mandapati**

   Poet of "Be Yours?"

   Sahithi has been a member of the community since 2021 and she writes poems. Her works can be accessed at writerspouch.com/profile/55

6. **Santhosh Annabattula**

   Poet of "Rower", "Sinner" & "Survivor"

   Santhosh has been a member of the community since 2011 and he writes poems & short stories. His works can be accessed at writerspouch.com/profile/3

About Photographers

1. **Krishna Guttikonda**

   Photographer for "See You Tomorrow" & "Sinner"

   Krishna has been a member of the community since 2021 and he contributes pictures. His contributions can be accessed at writerspouch.com/profile/58

2. **Manohar Koviri**

   Photographer for "My Anxiety Speaks to Me!"

   Manohar has been a member of the community since 2022 and he contributes pictures. His contributions can be accessed at writerspouch.com/profile/64

3. **Nikhil Narayanasa**

   Photographer for "Whispers & Murmurs"

   Nikhil has been a member of the community since 2015 and he contributes poems & pictures. His contributions can be accessed at writerspouch.com/profile/17

4. **Pankaj Tottada**

   Photographer for "Beads", "Be Yours?", "Realisation", "Rower", &

"Survivor"

Pankaj has been a member of the community since 2015 and he has contributed numerous photographs. His contributions can be accessed at writerspouch.com/profile/13

5. **Prabhath Narapareddy**

   Photographer for "Delight" & "The Lonely Heart's Stupid Song"

   Prabhath has been a member of the community since 2014 and he contributes photographs. His contributions can be accessed at writerspouch.com/profile/7

6. **Ravindra Patoju**

   Photographer for "Grey"

   Ravindra has been a member of the community since 2020 and he contributes photographs. His contributions can be accessed at writerspouch.com/profile/38

About Community

Writers Pouch is an Indian community that commissions various works of different art forms. Encompassing creators, contributors, editors, proofreaders, reviewers, photographers, and illustrators, the organisation aims to create unique forms of art in every genre.

Established in 2009, Writers Pouch started by publishing short stories, essays and poems. Later on, the organisation even started releasing novelettes, novellas, novels, book series, & non-fiction.

The goal of Writers Pouch is to explore art uniquely and this is accomplished by commissioning a group of artists on every project. They are a home for all creative individuals who are striving to tell their stories or ideas creatively while holding on to their principles.

If you loved our works, visit our website at writerspouch.store to buy our other titles:

1. I'm Your Loving Intern [2015]
2. Loving Intern [2016]
3. The Soul Snatchers [2016]
4. Broken Bonds [2017]
5. God's Council: The Four Auins [2017]
6. Your Loving Intern [2018]
7. Eternal Bond [2019]

8. Burning Beacons [2020]
9. A Walk in Paradise [2020]
10. Immortal Verses [2020]
11. Eccentric Endings [2020]
12. Casket of Tales [2020]
13. Whispering Thoughts [2021]
14. Radical Realities [2021]
15. Strange Lives [2021]
16. Callous Conclusions [2021]
17. His Past & Her Future [2021]
18. Creators' Memoirs [2021]
19. The Soul Snatcher [2022]

9 798885 918701

Printed by Libri Plureos GmbH in Hamburg,
Germany